What on Earth!

What are you interested in? This might be the most important question you ever ask yourself. All our books at What on Earth! are designed to help you explore and discover whatever fascinates you most. And when you share your discoveries with others, your joy spreads far and wide. Because, when it comes right down to it... *the real world is far more amazing than anything you can make up!*

Christopher Lloyd
Founder, What on Earth!

1822

SPRING

Pairs of bald eagles soar carefree
and take rest in their nests
in loblolly pine trees.
As the cold heart of winter
melts into spring,
signs of life explode
among the wild and free things.

To my mother and my first grandchild,
to everything we seek to nurture in the wild,
to all children looking for ways to cope,
I dedicate Harriet's story, a song of hope.

– **Caroline Brewer**

HARRIET TUBMAN

Force of Nature

A biography in poems

Caroline Brewer

What on Earth!

TABLE OF CONTENTS

1822

BORN DAY

Beyond a little river
on oak-covered land,
a baby rocks in a cradle
carved by hand
from a sweet gum tree.
Araminta Ross
is born enslaved.
Born enslaved is she.
Yet nobody knows that this one birth
in Dorchester County, Maryland,
the United States, planet Earth,
starts a new chapter in world history.

WHAT SLAVERY SAYS

The American slavery system
says this baby girl
does not belong to her parents.
Says she
does not belong to herself.
Says this newborn child,
because she is Black,
belongs to someone else:
an enslaver.

Yet somehow Minty will know
that she
is soil, seed, root, tree,
stem, flower, air, breeze,
stream, river, waves, sea,
sun, moon, a planetary jubilee,
a meteor shower
causing darkness to flee.
Same as the eagles,
she was born free –
the way God intended
all of nature to be.

1822–1827

CHILD'S PLAY

Beautiful, brown, dainty, chocolate-eyed Minty
with her bushy black, wild and wonderful hair aplenty,
is outdoors, twirling, dancing,
running, laughing, prancing,
playing with seashells and sticks
until just before the age of six.

1827

THE END OF PLAY

The slavery system is so cruel,
Minty never gets a chance at school.
No nurturing to learn to read and write.
Hard labour is the young one's plight.

When Minty is hired out,
snatched from her mum and dad,
she's like a flower being
ripped from its garden bed.

MUSKRAT MISERY

Minty's new life
grows bleaker and bleaker.
She's alone collecting traps
with dying creatures.
Found on riverbanks and marshes,
they are flat-tailed, fat,
short-legged rodents
known as muskrats.
She trudges barefoot
through water so cold
it nearly freezes the life
out of her soul.

HOME,
WHERE THE HEALING IS

Minty is miserable, sick and weak.
She catches the measles.
Her mama rises to speak,

rumbling like a volcano,
lava spilling over her peak.
Rit demands her child be sent back to her arms,
to be wrapped in her love and healing charms.

Rit heals Minty with kindness and care,
herbs from the forest, and old-fashioned prayer.

1835

INNER VISIONS

Minty is thirteen. Pops into the Bucktown store.
Ready to buy goods as part of her chores.
A Black boy child is dashing towards the door,
refusing to be anybody's slave any more.

The overseer tries to stop him cold.
Throws a heavy iron weight.
But, lo and behold,
it hits Minty in the head.
Breaks her skull, she says.
Takes chunks of her breath.
She reels at the edge of death.

Afterwards, deep sleeping spells come.
The enslaver thinks she's worthless.
Some children think she's dumb.
Because on any given day,
sitting or standing, she drifts away.

This is when God is holding Minty's hand,
leading her through visions
of the Promised Land,
floating in outer space, among the stars,
finding her place beyond slavery's prison bars.

UNCHAINED

Shhhhh...
Every now and then,
Minty and her brothers,
Henry and Ben,
take the liberty
to visit their parents' plantations secretly.

On these 15-mile round trips,
by foot, wagon and boat,
hope for better days catches in their throats.

THE MELLOW MARSH

Along the way, marshes provide a space
for nature to burst out all over the place.
Tundra swans, white as clouds, whistle and float.
Canada geese and snow geese quack and rattle their throats.
Mallard ducks and black ducks glide from side to side.
Diamondback turtles mostly stay underwater and hide.
Great blue herons hunt in broad daylight.
Fowler's toads buzz and trill at night.
Spotted salamander bodies twist and jerk
across grass, leaves and watery earth.

WOODLANDS
AND WATERWAYS

Minty's father is a timber supervisor.
From him, and her mama, she learns
to be wiser
about the ways of the woods
and trees.
How to stay alive.
How even to thrive
among oak, maple, walnut, pine
– just a few of the common kind.

Five feet tall and strong,
Minty matches the men all day long,
chopping trees, hustling, grinding,
sweat pouring, hot sun shining.

She also rides a mule, slogging logs
across grassy ground.
To Stewart's Canal, the pair are bound.
From there, timber will float
without need of a boat
to Tobacco Stick Bay
and be sold upriver in the coming days.

RANAWAY the 17th
RANAWAY the 17th
THREE chestnut
about 27 years, is
HUNDRED DOLLAR
REWARD. reward
RANAWAY high; MINTY, aged
the 17th a chestnut color, fine
high; MINTY, aged about 27 years, i
a chestnut color, fine looking, and abou
feet high. One hundred dollars rewar
will be given for each of the above name
groes, if taken out of the State, and $50 e
taken in the State. They must be lodg
5 feet 8 or 9 inches high; BEN, aged age
bout 25 years, is very quick to speak when
They must be lodged in
BEN, aged about

BLACK JACKS ALONG THE BAY

Minty labours along Tobacco Stick Bay,
and meets Black Jacks working the waterways
up, down and all around,
with access to big cities and small towns.
These Black sailors are free;
they network for enslaved communities;
share information on escape opportunities.
They know who to talk to and who not,
so that those heading North can avoid getting caught.
For Minty, a thrilling new world
is being unfurled.

1844

NEW VOWS

Minty, in her early 20s,
takes her mother's first name.
As Harriet, she enters a time
of radical change.

She also says yes
to John Tubman,
a free Black man
who asks to be her husband.
To his moon, she is the sun,
enough light for him and everyone.

When John marries Harriet,
major freedoms are taken away.
Any children they have
will be born enslaved.
They could be stolen from them any day.
Harriet also could be sold away.
John Tubman would have no say.

All of him had to love all of her
to imagine he might turn the tide
of slavery's family apartheid.

1849

STEALING AWAY

With rumours she'll be sold in late 1849,
Harriet makes a play for freedom for the first time.
Ben and Henry agree
they are willing as well to take off to be free.

Harriet begs her husband, John, to come.
But he's not willing to go on the run.
Her heart breaks in two.
Emotions go to war over what to do.
And yet, Harriet knows she must break the chains
and hop on board the freedom train.

So off she and her brothers go,
facing dangers they know of
and those they don't know.
After two weeks,
fear sucks the life from her brothers' bravery.
They drag themselves – and Harriet –
back into slavery.

1849

SECRET JUBILATION

Early October, Harriet stamps out all doubt.
Declares, again, she's heading out.
She sings herself right off the plantation,
hoping the community celebrates in hush-hush jubilation.
She sets out alone for the Underground Railroad,
that secret network of people, paths and codes.
As the seed of freedom, she's eager to be sowed.

THE SKY IN HER EYES

Travelling at night, Harriet reads the sky.
Since childhood, she's held its brilliance in her eyes.
Among the trillions of stars way up,
Harriet spies the edge of the Big Dipper's cup,
pointing down to Polaris, the North Star,
which shows the way to go from wherever we are.
It always beams from roughly the same place,
blanketing Harriet with a feeling of grace.
She knows that the steady star's light
will escort her to freedom's delight.

SILENT AS THE OWL

Like the owl flapping its wings
with a swishing sort of hush,
mimicking the silky sound of a drummer's brush,
Harriet makes soft, near silent, moves by night,
then hides herself from most in broad daylight.

1849

OH, OH, FREEDOM!

After three weeks on the run,
Harriet's feet are about done.
Her belly growls.
Sleep barks and howls.
Her body begs to be scrubbed;
to soak way down deep in a tub.

A grassy meadow appears,
voice calling: 'Enter here, my dear.'
Stepping on Pennsylvania, free land,
basking in the sun's warm, golden strands,
Harriet takes a fresh look at her hands.
Asks if she's still the same woman.
And whether that's Heaven across the field?
Yes... Harriet's feet are worn,
but her soul is happy and healed.

FREEDOM-BOUND, UNDERGROUND

Freedom-seeking, now in Harriet's bones,
is like the fire the Bible's Jeremiah had known,
the one he said wouldn't leave him alone.

Missing family and friends,
she heads South again
to keep slavery's brutality
from devouring her kin.

NO TURNING BACK

The first group moves out to silent, happy shouts.

Soon, shoes get tattered, feet get battered.
Clothing sags, turns to near rags.
They trek over spiky sweetgum balls,
causing cuts so painful they stumble and fall.

And yet these folks who are freedom-bound
trust their Moses will keep them safe and sound.
Come rain, sleet, snow or frozen ground,
won't let nobody or nothing turn them around.

MUSIC IN THE AIR

Lots of escapes occur in winter,
when most forms of food are rare,
and bodies plead desperately
for more than water and air.
To feed their souls, as well,
Harriet loves to sing.
Her treasure chest of spirituals
makes the bells of possibility ring.

As welcome as birdsong, Harriet warbles,
'Bound for the Promised Land',
to lift the spirits of every child, woman and man.

She sings, 'Tell old Pharaoh to let my people go!'
when they should stay off the main roads.

To call her passengers out of hiding,
she croons, 'Hail, oh, hail, ye happy spirits',
in a voice just loud enough
for them to hear it.

FOOD FOR
THE HUNGRY

Finding enough food is always a strain,
yet nature, in every season,
has supplies for the human train.
Harriet has been raised to forage,
so she dips into her store of courage
and goes on solo missions to scoop
nuts, berries and pawpaw fruit
to help them stay strong
so they have energy to push further on.

PRAYER CHANGES THINGS

Harriet makes the time
to travel to a sacred place in her mind
to pray among the wild things.
Or sometimes, she just drops,
because of that head injury,
and fades off into visions and dreams,
where the voice of God is always supreme.

When she was a child
her people would retreat to the wild
to pray, sing, dance
and be whisked off into a trance;
into shrieks, wails, moans, hums,
some going limp until clarity comes
washing over them like gentle rain
after the wind of a gospel hurricane.

She and God talk like old friends.
And after the spiritual voyage ends,
she resumes her story or quest again,
as naturally as nature's sweet rhythms.

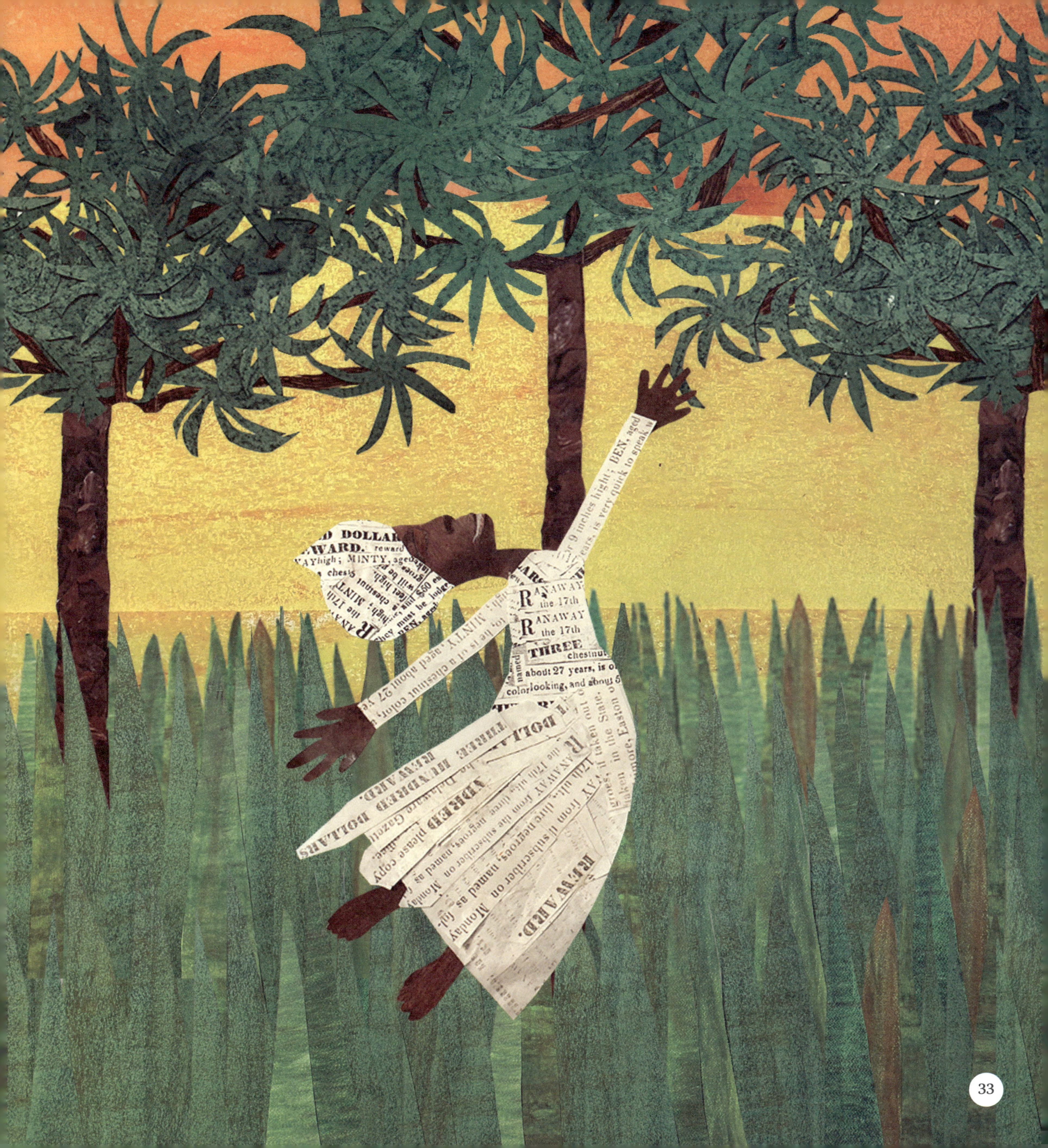

WADE IN THE WATER

Freedom-seekers in the woods,
getting away, feeling good.
Then, God tells Harriet
for their protection
she must turn in a different direction.

They face a river –
no boat to ride,
no place to cross,
or run or hide.

Following Harriet,
they wade in,
face the fear –
they cannot swim –
flowing with the water's skin,
breathing out, breathing in,
soaking wet to the chin.

They reach the shore, then liberty's golden door.
Harriet's passengers could not adore her more.

UP FROM THE UNDERGROUND

After her thirteenth trip to unchain her folks,
Harriet lets go of pines, maples and oaks –
corn fields, roosters, pigs, cows –
cardinals, blue jays, barred owls –
streams, rivers, ocean, bays –
swamps, forests, hideaways –
night crawling, secret codes:
life on the blessed Underground Railroad.

THE CIVIL WAR COMES TO HARRIET'S DOOR

A battle begins between the states.
To end slavery, or not, is what's at stake.
The Union Army calls Harriet out of retirement.
To be a scout and a spy is the requirement:
to map out plans for escapes and attacks,
to sneak behind the enemy's back,
to talk to the enslaved in disguise,
to work for freedom as bullets fly,
to be as dazzling
in intelligence gathering
as a purple sunrise.

THE MERCY
OF A SUNSET

And yet Harriet is asked to do more
than be a spy during the war.
Into the battlefield
she's implored to swoop
to be a nurse for Black Army troops.
But the military does not pay
this angel of mercy for her workdays.
So she's forced to earn money by hook or by crook
using skills as a laundress, seamstress and cook.

As the elders like to say,
this is Harriet 'making a way out of no way',
showing up like an orange sunset
near the end of the day.

THE COMBAHEE FREE

Of course, this making-a-way thing is not new.
For Harriet's whole life, it's been her truth.
She is the first woman, in 1863,
to lead armed soldiers of the military.
Confederates plant bombs in the Combahee River,
enough to make a rescue party shiver.
But Harriet helps the Black soldiers
detect all the floating mines.
They land their boats in just the nick of time.

Like a tornado, they come in and rip
more than seven hundred people from slavery's grip.
Everything people can bring, they bring –
babies and children who cry and cling,
squealing pigs in sacks on their backs
(folks are making tracks and not looking back),
blankets and chickens clutched in their hands,
freshly cooked meals straight from the pan –
deliciously noisy as a marching band,
doing what they've got to do to grab liberty's hand.

1869–1913

LEGACY

Shortly after the Civil War,
veteran Nelson Davis becomes a boarder
at Harriet's final home in Auburn, New York.
In 1869, they become husband and wife,
nurturing gardens and farms
as they build their new life.

An apple orchard is already on the property.
Nelson helps Harriet expand it with new apple trees.
She shares her homegrown bounty, generously.
Children and those formerly enslaved are the primary beneficiaries.

Harriet's legacy has this one grand feature:
loving and uplifting all of God's creatures.

A FORCE OF NATURE

From the dawn of her life,
Harriet knew that she
was meant to be
soil, seed, root, tree,
stem, flower, air, breeze,
stream, river, waves, sea,
sun, moon, a planetary jubilee,
a meteor shower
causing darkness to flee.
Same as the eagles,
she was born free –
the way God intended
all of nature to be.

GLOSSARY

Adore – Love

Apartheid – A system that requires people be separated by race

Codes – A set of signals understood by only a limited group of people

Devouring – Swallowing hungrily

Healed – Brought back to health

History – The retelling of important events that happened in the past

Hustling – Hurrying

Jubilation – Extreme happiness

Jubilee – Celebration

Liberty – Freedom

Meteor shower – When a lot of meteors (also known as shooting stars) appear to come from one spot in the sky at about the same time

Mimicking – Copying

Nature – The aspects of the world that humans cannot make

Network – A group of connected people or things

Nurturing – Care or support

Overseer – Person given authority over those enslaved

Planetary – Huge; relating to the whole Earth or to another planet or planets

Plantation – A large piece of land farmed by paid or unpaid workers

Prison – A place where people are held against their will

Promised Land – Heaven, or a place where God promises his people's suffering will ease or end

Retreat – Withdraw to a quiet or safe place

Slavery – The practice of owning and controlling other humans as if they were animals or objects, including taking them from their homes, buying and selling them, forcing them to work without rest, and abusing them both physically and mentally

Spirituals – Emotional religious songs developed by enslaved people in the United States

Trance – A state so intense that the person in a trance isn't aware of their surroundings

Trill – A sound made by moving quickly back and forth between two tones

Unfurled – Unfolded or unrolled

Veteran – A former soldier

A NOTE ON THE ILLUSTRATIONS

Though I have written several books, this is my very first time illustrating one. I used collage – including cut paper of several types, natural objects and photos – and drew on them with oil pastels, coloured pencils, chalk, markers and a little acrylic paint. I used newsprint to make the clothing of enslaved people to show that they – and enslavement generally – were always, and still are, important news. Thanks to Danielle Brewer, Diane Brewer, Glenn Brewer, Marcus Brewer, Sani Daniella Brewer-Wimes, Alex Dorisca, Chloe Dorisca, Christian Dorisca, Lendell Dorisca, George Eldridge, Jr., George Eldridge, Sr., Lavraeae Eldridge, Jabari Exum, Laniyah Harvin, Cameron Howard, Elizabeth Howard, Genae Howard, Navi Howard, Tykara Howard, Naszir Love, and Karen Wilson-Ama'Echefu for sharing their family photos with me so I could use them along with my own as models for some of the people in the book.

It is my amazing good fortune that my brother, Glenn Brewer, is a professional illustrator, and he agreed to draw the animals and plants that were beyond my abilities (I did the trees and the grass, though). Our cousin George Eldridge, Photoshop wizard, came to the rescue in the next stage. He uploaded all of the pieces I had collaged, and we worked together to arrange them into full scenes. Brilliant art director Bea Jackson shepherded me through the whole process, giving feedback on every element of the illustrations. Responding to her comments always elevated the art. Thank you, Glenn, George and Bea! I couldn't have done it without you.

CANADA

Lake Huron

ONTARIO

Lake Ontario NEW YORK

Lake Erie

NEW HAMP-SHIRE   MAINE

VERMONT

MASSACHUSETTS

RHODE ISLAND

CONNECTICUT

PENNSYLVANIA

NEW JERSEY

U N I T E D   S T A T E S

OHIO

MARYLAND

DELAWARE

WASHINGTON, DC

WEST VIRGINIA
(part of Virginia until 1863)

VIRGINIA

KENTUCKY

TENNESSEE

NORTH CAROLINA

SOUTH CAROLINA

GEORGIA

A HARRIET TUBMAN MAP

✖ **St. Catharines, Ontario, Canada** – A small community of newly free Blacks where Harriet settled with her brothers and parents beginning in the mid 1850s after the 1850 Fugitive Slave Law was enacted in the United States.

⬠ **Auburn, New York** – Where Harriet brought her parents, brothers, nephews and nieces and lived from 1859 until her death in 1913.

❖ **Baltimore, Maryland** – Home to a network of free Blacks, including many sailors called Black Jacks, who shared information about the geography of the East Coast and how the enslaved could free themselves using waterways.

✦ **Cape May, New Jersey** – Where Harriet lived and worked as a cook during the summers of 1850, 1851 and 1852, saving up money in between Underground Railroad trips.

✺ **Dorchester County, Maryland** – Home to an abundance of fish, crustaceans and wetlands; where Harriet was born into captivity and grew up, longing for freedom.

◆ **Philadelphia, Pennsylvania** – Where Harriet met William Still, considered Father of the Underground Railroad, became an official conductor on the UGRR, and lived and worked for several years after freeing herself.

■ **Beaufort, South Carolina** – Where Harriet served as cook, nurse, scout and spy for the Union Army during the Civil War and led the raid of several plantations along the Combahee River, helping 756 enslaved people secure freedom.

HISTORICAL PHOTOS

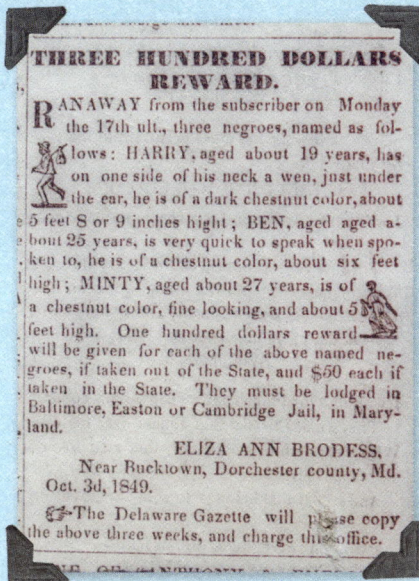

This newspaper ad offered a reward for anyone who helped capture Harriet (here called Minty) and her brothers when they first escaped enslavement in 1849 *(see page 23)*.

Cabins where enslaved people on a rice plantation along the Combahee River used to live, before Harriet and her band of Union troops freed them *(see page 38)*. The cabins are still there, though nobody lives in them any more.

Muskrats *(see page 11)* live in wetlands all over the USA and Canada and in Northern Mexico, too. In Harriet's time, they were hunted mostly for their fur, which was used to make fur coats and hats.

There are no photos of Harriet working in a Civil War army camp, but here is a Union Army soldier watching over cooking pots, as Harriet would have done *(see page 37)*.

Harriet Tubman, her husband Nelson Davis and their adopted daughter Gertie Davis at their home in Auburn, New York, in the 1880s *(see page 41)*.

Harriet in 1911, at the age of 89.

SOURCE NOTES

This book was developed through extensive, relentless and joyful research over three years, including many interviews, thousands of pages of books, studies and articles, and eight visits to the wonderful Harriet Tubman sites on the Eastern Shore of Maryland (the part of the state east of the Chesapeake Bay).

Alan Spears, a historian for the National Parks Conservation Foundation, was key to getting the research process underway by helping me realize the incredible breadth of Harriet's understanding of the natural world. Spears introduced me to Dana Paterra, then Manager of the Harriet Tubman Underground Railroad State Park and Visitor Center, who generously answered every question I posed over three years and led me on a four-hour tour of the Harriet Tubman Byway.

I walked a portion of the former Anthony Thompson plantation, where Harriet is believed to have been born, and peeked into several windows of the still-standing Bucktown store.

In Caroline County, I strolled among fruit and nut trees on Mount Pleasant Acres Farm and through the adjacent small forest. This land is now owned by Paulette Green and Donna Dear, who are preserving it for its historical significance. It's where Harriet's parents were living when she helped them escape in 1857. Walking where Harriet once walked, where her parents once lived, where faith dreams took flight in the middle of cold, dark nights, with big, tall trees as silent witnesses, sent chills down my spine.

I cruised through the Blackwater National Wildlife Refuge (BNWR) one winter, stopping to watch flocks of ducks and geese, and exchanged emails with a BNWR staff member about the wildflowers that would have been abundant during Harriet's time. I also toured Adkins Arboretum with the impressive historian Anthony Cohen, Founder of Button Farm Living History Center, one spring to see plants and fruit and nut trees like those that helped Harriet and other freedom-seekers survive.

The generous and thoughtful Kate Clifford Larson, considered the definitive biographer of Tubman and expert consultant for this book, and Linda Harris, co-director of the Harriet Tubman Museum and Educational Center in Cambridge, Maryland, and a force of nature, music and history herself, were very generous with their time and expertise. I attended book talks by historian Edda L. Fields-Black, author of the remarkable, elucidating book *Combee*. *Combee* and the intensely compelling *Night Flyer* and *Wild Girls* by historian Tiya Miles were published after I had written the almost final draft of this book, but each of them helped me to tighten my storytelling and visual depictions and to gain a more solid grasp on the incredible environmental and spiritual life of Harriet Tubman.

I'm exceedingly grateful to everyone… and to my mother, who has encouraged me, in every endeavour, all of my life. They say that an author is only as good as her sources. And in my case, my inspirations have mattered a great deal as well.

SELECTED BIBLIOGRAPHY

Adkins Arboretum. https://www.adkinsarboretum.org/about_us/

Clinton, Catherine. *Harriet Tubman: The Road to Freedom*. Back Bay Books/Little Brown & Company, 2004

Fields-Black, Edda L. *Combee: Harriet Tubman, the Combahee Raid, and Black Freedom During the Civil War*. Oxford University Press, 2024

Harriet Tubman's Auburn Home. https://www.harriettubmanhome.com/

Harriet Tubman Underground Railroad National Historical Park. https://www.nps.gov/hatu/planyourvisit/hours.htm

Harriet Tubman Underground Railroad Scenic Byway and All-American Road. https://harriettubmanbyway.org/

Harriet Tubman Underground Railroad State Park and Visitor Center. https://dnr.maryland.gov/publiclands/Pages/eastern/tubman.aspx

Larson, Adam. 'Harriet Tubman in Baltimore', *Maryland Department of Natural Resources*. https://news.maryland.gov/dnr/2022/02/01/harriet-tubman-in-baltimore/

Larson, Kate Clifford. *Bound for the Promised Land: Harriet Tubman, Portrait of an American Hero*. One World, Random House, 2003

Larson, Kate Clifford. *Harriet Tubman Underground Railroad National Monument Historic Resource Study* (in partnership with the Organization of American Historians). National Park Service, 2019

Miles, Tiya. *Night Flyer: Harriet Tubman and the Faith Dreams of a Free People*. Penguin Press, 2024

Miles, Tiya. *Wild Girls: How the Outdoors Shaped the Women Who Challenged a Nation*. W.W. Norton & Company, 2023

Still, William. *The Underground Railroad: Authentic Narratives and First-Hand Accounts*. Dover Publications, 2007

INDEX

What on Earth!

What on Earth! is an imprint of What on Earth Publishing
The Black Barn, Wickhurst Farm, Leigh, Tonbridge, Kent, UK, TN11 8PS
30 Ridge Road Unit B, Greenbelt, Maryland, 20770, United States

First published in the United Kingdom in 2025

Designed by Bea Jackson
Expert consultant: Kate Clifford Larson
Image credits: **p. 44 map base** ii-graphics / Adobe Stock ; **p. 45 top left** Maurice Savage / Alamy Stock Photo; **p. 45 top centre** Andrew Lichtenstein / Corbis News / Getty Images; **p. 45 top right** Judy Tomlinson / 500px / Getty Images; **p. 45 bottom left** Keen Collection / Archive Photos / Getty Images; **p. 45 bottom centre** Heritage Images / Hulton Archive / Getty Images; **p. 45 bottom right** Universal History Archive / Universal Images Group / Getty Images.

About the type: The text is set in Adriane Text, a typeface designed by Marconi Gomes Lima of Typefolio, a Brazilian type foundry. Titles are set in Sunshine Daisies Serif, designed by Elena Genova.

Staff for this book: Nancy Feresten, Managing Director and Editor; Natalie Bellos, Publisher; Andy Forshaw, Art Director; Casey Neumann, Managing Editor; Alison Eldridge and Charka Stout, Proofreaders; Sian Smith, Production Manager

A CIP catalogue record for this book is available from the British Library

ISBN: 9781804661437

Printed in Malaysia

VC/Rawang, Malaysia/03/2025

10 9 8 7 6 5 4 3 2 1

whatonearthbooks.com

MIX
Paper | Supporting responsible forestry
FSC® C084469